A Note From Rick Renner

I am on a personal quest to see a "revival of the Bible" so people can establish their lives on a firm foundation that will stand strong and endure the test when the end-time storm winds begin to intensify.

In order to experience a revival of the Bible in your personal life, it is important to take time each day to read, receive, and apply its truths to your life. James tells us that if we will continue in the perfect law of liberty — refusing to be forgetful hearers but determined to be doers — we will be blessed in our ways. As you watch or listen to the programs in this series and work through this corresponding study guide, I trust that you will search the Scriptures and allow the Holy Spirit to help you hear something new from God's Word that applies specifically to your life. I encourage you to be a doer of the Word that He reveals to you. Whatever the cost, I assure you — it will be worth it.

> Thy words were found, and I did eat them;
> and thy word was unto me the joy and rejoicing of mine heart:
> for I am called by thy name, O Lord God of hosts.
> — Jeremiah 15:16

Your brother and friend in Jesus Christ,

Rick Renner

Insights on Communion

Copyright © 2020 by Rick Renner
8316 E. 73rd St.
Tulsa, Oklahoma 74133

Published by Rick Renner Ministries
www.renner.org

ISBN 13: 978-1-68031-676-6

eBook ISBN 13: 978-1-68031-681-0

How To Use This Study Guide

This five-lesson study guide corresponds to *"Insights on Communion" With Rick Renner* (Renner TV). Each lesson in this study guide covers a topic that is addressed during the program series, with questions and references supplied to draw you deeper into your own private study of the Scriptures on this subject.

To derive the most benefit from this study guide, consider the following:

First, watch or listen to the program prior to working through the corresponding lesson in this guide. (Programs can also be viewed at **renner.org** by clicking on the Media/Archives links.)

Second, take the time to look up the scriptures included in each lesson. Prayerfully consider their application to your own life.

Third, use a journal or notebook to make note of your answers to each lesson's Study Questions and Practical Application challenges.

Fourth, invest specific time in prayer and in the Word of God to consult with the Holy Spirit. Write down the scriptures or insights He reveals to you about being filled with the Spirit and empowered by Him in your daily life.

Finally, take action! Whatever the Lord tells you to do according to His Word, do it.

For additional study material, it is recommended that you obtain Denise Renner's book *Redeemed From Shame*. You may also select from Rick's available resources by placing your order at **renner.org** or by calling 1-800-742-5593.

TOPIC

Components of a Covenant

SCRIPTURES

1. **Hebrews 6:13, 14, 17** — For when God made promise to Abraham, because he could swear by no greater, he sware by himself, saying, Surely blessing I will bless thee, and multiplying I will multiply thee. Wherein God, willing more abundantly to shew unto the heirs of promise the immutability of his counsel, confirmed it by an oath.

2. **1 Corinthians 11:27-30** — Wherefore whosoever shall eat this bread, and drink this cup of the Lord, unworthily, shall be guilty of the body and blood of the Lord. But let a man examine himself, and so let him eat of that bread, and drink of that cup. For he that eateth and drinketh unworthily, eateth and drinketh damnation to himself, not discerning the Lord's body. For this cause many are weak and sickly among you, and many sleep.

3. **1 Samuel 18:3, 4** — Then Jonathan and David made a covenant, because he loved him as his own soul. And Jonathan stripped himself of the robe that was upon him, and gave it to David, and his garments, even to his sword, and to his bow, and to his girdle.

GREEK WORDS

1. "sware" — ὀμνύω (*omnuo*): to make an unbreakable promise

2. "by himself" — καθ' ἑαυτοῦ (*kath heautou*): by himself; on the basis of himself; according to himself

3. "oath" — ὅρκος (*horkos*): an oath that fences one in; an oath that perpetually binds; an oath from which there is no way out

SYNOPSIS

The five lessons in this study entitled *Insights on Communion* will focus on the following topics:

- Components to a Covenant

- What Is the Significance of Communion to You and Me?

- A Gospel-by-Gospel Comparison of Communion
- What Does It Mean To Be Guilty of the Blood and Body of Jesus?
- The Supernatural Element in Communion

The emphasis of this lesson:

The nine components of a covenant are: covenant promises, a blood sacrifice, a bloody path, blessings and curses, the mingling of blood, the exchange of names, an exchange of gifts, a covenant meal, and a memorial event.

On the night Jesus was betrayed into the hands of the religious leaders, He shared one final Passover meal with His disciples. With that meal, He served them what we have come to know as *Communion*. In those sacred moments, Jesus and His disciples entering into covenant with each other. In the same way, when we partake of Communion today, we enter into covenant with Christ personally and reaffirm the eternal covenant God made with us through His Son Jesus Christ. Understanding what a covenant is and what it means is foundational to understanding and truly appreciating Communion.

THE NINE COMPONENTS OF A COVENANT

Component One: Covenant Promises

There are four primary reasons for choosing to enter into a covenant partnership with someone. These include a desire for relationship, protection, trust, and love. When two parties enter into a covenant, it guarantees each of them can expect faithfulness, loyalty, and dependability from the other. In the Old Testament, they also made promises to each other, and the covenant they established extended to many generations. We see this in the example of the covenant made between David and Saul's son Jonathan (*see* 1 Samuel 20:16,17).

In the Old Testament, when you made a covenant with an individual, it meant you also honored it with his family for up to *seven* generations. The number seven symbolized forever. When Jonathan died, David's covenant with him extended to his grandson Mephibosheth. For Jonathan's sake,

David cared for and treated Mephibosheth like royalty. This lets us know covenants are a serious matter and they are to be kept.

Component Two: A Blood Sacrifice

In every covenant, there was always some kind of *blood sacrifice*. The word for "covenant" in Hebrew literally means *to cut until the blood flows*. There could be no covenant without the shedding of blood. The words "to cut a covenant" refers to cutting until the blood flows.

Normally, when a covenant was cut, an animal would be cut down the backbone, and the two halves of the carcass were placed side by side to form a wall of blood, leaving a path of blood on the ground in between the pieces. This is seen in Genesis 15 when Abraham killed an assortment of animals and placed their halves in position to prepare for making a covenant with God. These were the blood sacrifice. Interestingly, the reason Abraham was called the "friend of God" was because God entered into a covenant with him.

Component Three: A Bloody Path

In order for there to be a blood sacrifice, blood had to be shed. Once animals were sacrificed and their pieces laid out on the ground, the people making the covenant with each other often joined hands and walked through the pieces upon the bloody path. This symbolized both partners dying to self and becoming one. Often witnesses from both sides attended to watch the covenant-making event.

When God made His covenant with Abraham, Abraham sacrificed all the animals and placed their halves on the ground. As he waited for God to arrive, the Bible says, "…A deep sleep fell upon Abram; and lo, an horror of great darkness fell upon him" (Genesis 15:12). God brought an immobilizing sleep on Abram so that he could not move. Then a smoking furnace and a burning lamp passed through the pieces of the animals (*see* Genesis 15:17). These images represented the presence of God. Abram watched from his trance-like state as God Himself, *by Himself*, walked through the midst of the sacrificed animals. God made the covenant with Himself. This is what is known as the Abrahamic Covenant.

Hebrews 6:13 says, "For when God made promise to Abraham, because he could swear by no greater, he sware by himself." The word "sware" here is the Greek word *omnuo*, which means *to make an unbreakable promise*.

God made an unbreakable promise "by himself," which in the Greek literally means *by himself, on the basis of himself, according to himself.* No one else participated in the promise that was made.

God continued in the very next verse, "Saying, Surely blessing I will bless thee, and multiplying I will multiply thee" (Hebrews 6:14). Basically, God stood in the midst of those pieces, looked at Abraham and said, "I am bound and determined to bless you. I'm going to multiply you in spite of all the mistakes you have made. I Myself have chosen you."

In Hebrews 6:17, the writer went on to say, "Wherein God, willing more abundantly to shew unto the heirs of promise the immutability of his counsel, confirmed it by an oath." The word "oath" here in Greek is the word *horkos*, and it describes *an oath that fences one in; an oath that perpetually binds; an oath from which there is no way out.* This means God promised by His own name to never walk away from Abraham — regardless of what Abraham did.

Later, God did require Abraham to participate in the bloody side of the covenant through the act of circumcision. This cutting away of the flesh meant that every time Abraham saw himself privately, he was reminded of his covenant with God. It was an inescapable reminder in the most intimate area of who he was.

Component Four: Blessings and Curses

The partners cutting covenant together would pledge a never-ending commitment to each other, which included a continual flow of *blessings.* They would also acknowledge the *curses* of punishment for breaking the covenant. Most often, this was understood to be the curse of death that would come upon those who were unfaithful to a covenant.

This brings us to what the apostle Paul wrote about Communion in First Corinthians 11:27-30. He said, "Wherefore whosoever shall eat this bread, and drink this cup of the Lord, unworthily, shall be guilty of the body and blood of the Lord. But let a man examine himself, and so let him eat of that bread, and drink of that cup. For he that eateth and drinketh unworthily, eateth and drinketh damnation to himself, not discerning the Lord's body. For this cause many are weak and sickly among you, and many sleep."

In essence, this means if you don't keep your commitment in your covenant with God, you can reap negative consequences. This is what the Bible tells us with every single covenant that was ever made. The blessings connected to the covenant belonged to those who remained faithful to it.

Component Five: The Mingling of Blood

In every covenant there was always the *mingling of blood*. Blood in the Bible — and in many ancient cultures — symbolizes life. Leviticus 17:11 says, "For the life of the flesh is in the blood…." A covenant symbolizes taking in the blood of another and thereby acquiring that person's life. When someone gave their blood, it represented the giving of their life. Likewise, in a covenant, when someone took in the blood of another, it represented the taking in of their life.

There were a number of rituals for mingling the blood in the making of a covenant. In some cases, covenant partners would stand in the path of the blood that was spread on the ground from the sacrificed animal and then cut themselves and mingle their blood. Another custom was for covenant partners to put drops of each person's blood into a cup of wine, and then each partner would drink from it. A third common practice was for covenant partners to cut their palms and then entwine them together to mingle the blood.

By taking another person's blood, you literally became a partaker of that person's life and nature. In this way, two unrelated people could become one "flesh and blood." In the ancient world, this practice was often called "brothering" because it put two into a blood relationship of one. This was not a mere figure of speech. It was a very real and legal transaction that was not entered into lightly.

Component Six: The Exchange of Names

Along with the blood sacrifice, blessings and curses, and the mingling of blood, there was also a mingling or *exchange of names* to signify a covenant. Both partners might add the other's name to his or hers, or one might take on the other's name — a practice that is still common today in the covenant of marriage.

In the Old Testament, when God entered into covenant with Abram, He changed Abram's name to *Abraham*, and He changed Sarai's name to *Sarah*. Similarly, God changed Jacob's name to *Israel* and Saul to *Paul*.

Even Jesus — God in the flesh — changed Simon's name to *Peter*. We will see the importance of this in the lessons ahead.

Component Seven: An Exchange of Gifts

Not only were names exchanged between covenant partners, but also *gifts were exchanged*. We see this custom demonstrated in the covenant relationship between David and Jonathan. In First Samuel 18:3 and 4, the Bible says, "Then Jonathan and David made a covenant, because he loved him as his own soul. And Jonathan stripped himself of the robe that was upon him, and gave it to David, and his garments, even to his sword, and to his bow, and to his girdle."

What is interesting is that each of the items mentioned had significance. A person's robe represented the *identity* and *authority* of the person. When Jonathan gave David his robe, he was giving him his identity and authority. A sword represented *strength* and *protection*. By giving David his sword, Jonathan was saying, "I promise to use all my power to protect you." Finally, the girdle represented a person's *possessions* and their *wealth*. When Jonathan gave David his girdle, it was the same as saying, "Whatever I have is at your disposal."

Component Eight: A Covenant Meal

Along with the aforementioned elements, covenant partners typically shared *a covenant meal*. This consisted of bread and wine. The bread represented *flesh*. It was also symbolic of a person's *wealth* and *all that he or she possessed*. Covenant partners would take a loaf of bread and divide it in half, symbolizing the sharing of one another's resources. When people cut covenant and broke bread together, it was the equivalent of saying, "Everything I have is at your disposal."

Wine represented *blood*. Covenant partners could drink wine as a symbol of blood, giving their life to the other. Depending on the church, wine or juice is used in the taking of Communion. Both are produced by the crushing or squeezing of grapes, which depicts that life has been given; someone has sacrificed their life, shedding their blood to keep the covenant.

Bread was the promise of shared wealth and possessions, and wine symbolized the life's blood to empower the promise. The drinking of the cup was each participant's way of saying, "If I have to give my life to empower this covenant, I will give it. I will give everything I have to stand by the commitment I'm making to you this day."

Component Nine: A Memorial Event

One of the most important components of making a covenant was *a memorial event.* This was a reminder to all parties — and a visible witness — that a covenant had been made. Some examples of memorial events from Scripture include:

- **The rainbow** – God stretched a rainbow across the sky as a sign of the covenant He made with Noah and all the creatures of the earth that He would never destroy the earth again by a flood (*see* Genesis 9:8-17). Every time we see a rainbow, we are reminded of this covenant.

- **Circumcision** – The cutting away of the foreskin, or circumcision, was given as a sign of the Abrahamic Covenant (*see* Genesis 17).

- **The planting of trees** – Abraham planted a grove of trees in Beersheba as witness to the covenant he made with Abimelech (*see* Genesis 21).

- **Erecting a stone pillar** - Jacob and Laban erected a stone pillar as witness to their covenant (*see* Genesis 31).

There was always a memorial event or witness to the covenant that was made between covenant partners. Understanding these nine components of the covenant is very helpful in understanding Communion.

STUDY QUESTIONS

Study to shew thyself approved unto God, a workman that needeth not to be ashamed, rightly dividing the word of truth.
— 2 Timothy 2:15

1. When God made His "oath" to Abraham (*see* Hebrews 6:13-17), He swore by His own name that He would never, ever abandon Abraham or renege on His covenant with him. According to Galatians 3:13-18 and verse 26-29, how are you a recipient of the same blessings promised to Abraham? How does this level of commitment from God encourage you?

2. The word "covenant" in Hebrew literally means *to cut until the blood flows*. The book of Hebrews has much to say about the Blood. Carefully read these verses and identify the *power* and *indispensable importance* of the Blood of Jesus. How is His Blood vastly superior to the blood of animals?
   - **Hebrews 9:12-14**
   - **Hebrew 9:22**
   - **Hebrews 10:4, 10-14**
   - **Hebrews 10:19-22**

PRACTICAL APPLICATION

> **But be ye doers of the word, and not hearers only, deceiving your own selves.**
> **— James 1:22**

1. Before you began this lesson, what was your understanding of a *covenant*? What connection — if any — were you aware of between a *covenant* and *Communion*?

2. How often do you take Communion at your church? Do you look forward to it? If so, why?

3. Do you ever take Communion on your own — just you and the Lord? How about with your family? What have these experiences been like, and what have you most enjoyed about them?

4. When God made His covenant with Abraham, He put Abraham to sleep and walked through the pieces of the sacrificed animals *alone*. Thus, God made the covenant with Himself. Why do you think God did this — especially in light of the blessings and curses connected with cutting a covenant?

TOPIC

What Is the Significance of Communion to You and Me?

SCRIPTURES

1. **2 Peter 1:3, 4** — According as his divine power hath given unto us all things that pertain unto life and godliness, through the knowledge of him that hath called us to glory and virtue. Whereby are given unto us exceeding great and precious promises: that by these ye might be partakers of the divine nature, having escaped the corruption that is in the world through lust.

2. **Hebrews 9:12** — Neither by the blood of goats and calves, but by his own blood he entered in once into the holy place, having obtained eternal redemption for us.

3. **Colossians 1:14** — In whom we have redemption through his blood, even the forgiveness of sins.

4. **John 14:13, 14** — And whatsoever ye shall ask in my name, that will I do, that the Father may be glorified in the Son. If ye shall ask any thing in my name, I will do it.

5. **1 Corinthians 5:17** — Therefore if any man be in Christ, he is a new creature: old things are passed away; behold, all things are become new.

6. **Ephesians 6:10** — …be strong in the Lord, and in the power of his might.

7. **Philippians 4:13** — I can do all things through Christ which strengtheneth me.

8. **John 16:15** — All things that the Father hath are mine: therefore said I, that he shall take of mine, and shall shew it unto you.

9. **Romans 8:16, 17** — The Spirit itself beareth witness with our spirit, that we are the children of God. And if children, then heirs; heirs of God, and joint-heirs with Christ….

10. **Ephesians 1:13** — In whom ye also trusted, after that ye heard the word of truth, the gospel of your salvation: in whom also after that ye believed, ye were sealed with that holy Spirit of promise.

GREEK WORDS

1. "hath given" — **δωρέομαι** (*doreomai*): in this passage, past tense; to bequeath; to amply give; to generously donate; to fully supply

2. "all things" — **πάντα** (*panta*): all things; it's an all-encompassing term; nothing is excluded

3. "life" — **ζωή** (*zoe*): present life; life of all kinds, especially spiritual life

4. "godliness" — **εὐσέβεια** (*eusebeia*): particularly describes godliness and what is related to godlikeness

5. "given" — **δωρέομαι** (*doreomai*): to bequeath; to amply give; to generously donate; to fully supply

6. "exceeding great" — **μέγιστα** (*megista*): magnificent; stunning; impressive

7. "precious" — **τίμιος** (*timios*): of great value; of great worth

8. "promises" — **ἐπάγγελμα** (*epangelma*): pronouncements; promises

9. "partakers" — **κοινωνία** (*koinonia*): from the word **κοινός** (*koinos*), which refers to things that are common or mutually shared, such as property that jointly belongs to two or more people; the ideas of commonality or connectedness is intrinsic to the meaning of this word; when **κοινός** (koinos) develops into the word **κοινωνός** (koinonos), it conveys the ideas of engagement, involvement, fellowship, or participation

10. "escaped" — **ἀποφεύγω** (*apopheugo*): escaped from; separated from

11. "corruption" — **φθορά** (*phthora*): corruption; decay; decomposition; perishableness; rottenness

SYNOPSIS

The practice of receiving Communion originated with Christ Himself over 2,000 years ago in the upper room in Jerusalem. A careful study of the New Testament reveals from that moment forward, believers regularly began partaking of Communion as a part of their worship. Rather than being just a religious ritual, Communion had great significance then — and it still has significance now. Indeed, there is great meaning in the bread that we break and the cup from which we drink.

In our first lesson, we examined nine components of an ancient covenant. In most covenants there were covenant promises, a blood sacrifice, a bloody path, blessings and curses, a mingling of blood, a change of names, an exchange of gifts, a covenant meal, and finally, a memorial event. Let's review each of these components and see how each one applies to our walk of faith.

The emphasis of this lesson:

There is a powerful connection between the nine components of a covenant and the practice of taking Communion. All of these components can be identified in the new covenant Jesus made with us through the Cross, and all have significance in our relationship with Him.

HOW THE COMPONENTS OF A COVENANT APPLY TO YOU

The Significance of Covenant Promises

There are four primary reasons for choosing to enter into a covenant partnership with someone: to have relationship and obtain protection, trust, and love. These elements were guaranteed to those who cut covenant together. And with the covenant, there was an exchange of *promises*. This is seen today in the promises, or vows, husbands and wives make to each other when they enter marriage, which is based on the ancient tradition of cutting a covenant.

The Bible details for us the promises of Jesus, should we choose to enter into a covenant with Him. In addition to eternal life, we are promised everything we need for life and godliness. Second Peter 1:3 says, "According as his divine power hath given unto us all things that pertain unto life and godliness, through the knowledge of him that hath called us to glory and virtue."

When the Scripture says "hath given," it is the Greek word *dureomai*, which is past tense and means *to bequeath*; *to amply give*; *to generously donate*; or *to fully supply.* Jesus hath given unto us "all things," which is the Greek word *panta*, meaning *all things*; it is *all encompassing*; *nothing excluded.* The things He has given us pertain to "life" — the Greek word *zoe*, which indicates *present life*; *life of all kinds*; *especially spiritual life.* They also pertain to "godliness," which in Greek is the word *eusebeia*, which particularly describes *godliness and what is related to godlikeness*. This means Jesus has given us everything we need for this present life and our future life. This includes healing, deliverance, soundness, preservation, wholeness, and eternal salvation. Think about it. We have been given the Blood of Jesus, the Word of God, the power of the Holy Spirit, and Heaven itself!

Second Peter 1:4 goes on to say, "Whereby are given unto us exceeding great and precious promises: that by these ye might be partakers of the divine nature, having escaped the corruption that is in the world through lust." The word "given" here is again the Greek word *dureomai*, which is past tense and means *to bequeath*; *to amply give*; *to generously donate*; or *to fully supply*.

Jesus has fully supplied us with "exceeding great and precious promises." The words "exceeding great" in Greek describe something *magnificent, stunning, and impressive*. The word "precious" is the Greek word *timios*, which means *of great value*; *of great worth*. And the word "promises" is the Greek word *epanggelma*, which describes *pronouncements* or *promises*. God made stunning and magnificent promises when He entered into covenant with us through Jesus.

In fact, the Bible says that we are "partakers of the divine nature." The word "partakers" is from the Greek word *koinonia*, which is from the word *koinos*, and refers to *things that are common or mutually shared, such as property that jointly belongs to two or more people*. The idea of *commonality* or *connectedness* is *intrinsic* to the meaning of this word. When *koinos* develops into the word *koinonos*, it conveys the ideas of *engagement, involvement, fellowship,* or *participation*. Therefore, when Scripture says we are "partakers of the divine nature," it means *we mutually share the same nature with Christ*.

Verse 4 also tells us we have "…escaped the corruption that is in the world through lust." The word "escaped" is the Greek word *apopheugo*, which means *escaped from* or *separated from*. And the word "corruption" is the Greek word *phthora*, which describes *corruption*; *decay*; *decomposition*; *perishableness*; or *rottenness*. The use of these words tells us that when we accepted God's new covenant through Jesus, we were separated from the corruption and decay of the world and became mutual sharers in Christ's divine nature. This was made possible through His blood sacrifice.

The Significance of the Blood Sacrifice

In every covenant there was also a *blood sacrifice*. We saw that the word for "covenant" in Hebrew means *to cut until the blood flows*. Jesus, who was God in the flesh, made a covenant with us with His own blood. Hebrews 12:24 says He is the Mediator of the new covenant, which was completed with the sprinkling of His blood.

When Jesus hung on the Cross, He became the blood sacrifice — the Passover Lamb (*see* 1 Corinthians 5:7) — to not just cover our sins, to take our sins away. Hebrews 9:12 tells us, "Neither by the blood of goats and calves, but by his own blood he entered in once into the holy place, having obtained eternal redemption for us." Jesus really shed His own blood to pay the penalty for our sins.

The Significance of the Bloody Path

Of course with every blood sacrifice, there was *a bloody path* created. We see that this took place when Jesus gave His life for us. As His body was tightly fastened to the whipping post, the scourge of the Roman soldiers cut deep into His flesh, lacerating capillaries and veins and causing great amounts of blood to flow. From the whipping post to the place called Golgatha, the broken and pulverized body of our Savior dripped with blood, and as He carried His Cross, He walked in the path of His own blood.

And just as there were normally witnesses who watched as covenants were made between two parties, there were hundreds — perhaps even thousands — of people who stood watching as Jesus walked that road to Calvary. They saw Him as He walked along the path drenched with His own blood. Although they did not understand it, they were living witnesses of the new covenant God was cutting with Christ on behalf of all mankind.

The Significance of Blessings and Curses

A fourth component of ancient covenants was *blessings and curses*. Covenant partners would swear a solemn commitment to each other that came with blessings for honoring the covenant and curses for breaking it. If one broke a covenant, it called down the curse of death on himself.

When Christ saved us, He also blessed us. Ephesians 1:3 says, "Blessed be the God and Father of our Lord Jesus Christ, who hath blessed us with all spiritual blessings in heavenly places in Christ." Jesus has given His life to us, and we have given our lives to Him in reciprocation. This is the great exchange. We make a solemn oath to die to ourselves — to abandon independent living — and to become one with Him and to live under His Lordship.

The Significance of Mingling of Blood

We learned in our previous lesson that *life is in the blood* (*see* Leviticus 17:11). Although many people today do not have this revelation, it was believed in most early cultures. When someone gave their blood, they were literally giving their life. Those who partook of another's blood became a co-joiner or participant in that person's life.

The *mingling of blood* in a covenant symbolizes taking in the blood of another and thereby acquiring that person's life. In this way, two unrelated people become one "flesh and blood." In ancient cultures, there was a term for this exchange known as "brothering." When a person partook of another person's blood, he or she became a legal brother of that person. Similarly, when you received Jesus' Blood, you became His brother or sister through the new covenant. Jesus is our elder brother (*see* Romans 8:29).

If you think about it, you were spiritually reborn as a child of God when you repented of your sins and received Christ as your Lord and Savior. At the same time, you also received a spiritual blood transfusion. You gave Him your sinful, dying blood, and He gave you His perfect, living blood (*see* Hebrews 9:14). Colossians 1:14 confirms this saying, "In whom we have redemption through his blood, even the forgiveness of sins."

As a born-again child of God, the Holy Spirit indwells you, and Jesus' blood cleanses you. Even though your physical body may look the same, you are a new creation in Christ — the old has passed away and the new has come (*see* 2 Corinthians 5:17).

The Significance of Changing Names

Another important component of a covenant was the *changing of names*. When we received Jesus, He gave us His name to use! He said, "And whatsoever ye shall ask in my name, that will I do, that the Father may be glorified in the Son" (John 14:13). To make sure that we heard Him, Jesus said again in the very next verse, "If ye shall ask any thing in my name, I will do it" (John 14:14).

Friend, when we partook of Jesus' body and blood and entered into covenant with Him, we were given the Name that is far above every name (*see* Philippians 2:9), and in the Name of Jesus we can heal the sick, cast out devils, and call Heaven to earth. We can confidently pray in His Name — presenting all that He is — and receive all that we need according to His Word!

The Significance of Exchange of Gifts

There was also always an *exchange of gifts* in the making of a covenant. In our previous lesson, we saw how Jonathan and David made a covenant with each other, and Jonathan gave David his robe, his weapons, and his girdle. The robe represented his *identity* and *authority*; his weapons represented the gift of his *power* and *protection*; and his girdle signified the giving of *all his wealth and possessions*. It was the equivalent of saying, "Whatever I have is at your disposal."

Similarly, when we entered into covenant with Christ, He gave us His robe. That is, He gave us a new identity — His identity! Second Corinthians 5:17 says, "Therefore if any man be in Christ, he is a new creature: old things are passed away; behold, all things are become new."

Likewise, Jesus also gave us weapons and power! This is confirmed in Ephesians 6:10, which instructs us to, "...Be strong in the Lord, and in the power of his might." We also see it in Philippians 4:13, which declares, "I can do all things through Christ which strengtheneth me."

Christ has given us everything He has! Before He laid down His life, He said, "All things that the Father hath are mine: therefore said I, that he [the Holy Spirit] shall take of mine, and shall shew it unto you" (John 16:15). Everything Jesus has in His possession, you have access to. It is all at your disposal through His blood as you ask in His Name.

The Significance of the Covenant Meal

Covenant partners also shared a covenant meal together, which consisted of bread and wine. The bread represented a person's flesh as well as all that he or she possessed in wealth and material goods. Covenant partners would tear a loaf of bread in half and feed the pieces to each other, signifying the joining of their flesh.

Wine represented blood — the shedding of one's blood to keep the covenant. Covenant partners would often pour wine and intertwine their arms while drinking it. This symbolized the joining of life, blood, and spirit. It was the equivalent of saying, "I'm not just making you a verbal promise for total access to my possessions, my wealth, and all that I have. I'm putting my blood behind my words."

The covenant meal of bread and wine was powerful. Each element symbolically declared, "My body is your body; my blood is your blood, and we have become one in every way." As believers, *Communion* is our covenant meal. Jesus literally made a covenant with His disciples through Communion; it was not a mere ritual. Every component of that evening was the making of a real, legitimate covenant, and the disciples clearly understood what was happening.

When Jesus gave His disciples the bread, He symbolically gave them His flesh as well as all He possessed. It was the equivalent of Him saying, "All that I have is at your disposal; there is not one thing of Mine that I will withhold from you." Likewise, when Jesus shared the cup of wine with His disciples, He was giving them His life's blood. It was as if He were saying, "I am yours and I will give My blood to empower this covenant and My promises to you." The truth is, when *you* take Communion, Christ offers you everything He offered His disciples that night in the upper room. You are His disciple too, and all that He has is made available to you by the Holy Spirit.

The Significance of the Memorial Event

The final component of a covenant that we observed was the inclusion of *a memorial event* or a *witness*. This was something that was done to serve as a permanent reminder of the covenant that had been made. Examples of this custom from the Old Testament include the planting of trees, the erecting of a column, or the heaping up of stones.

When it comes to the new covenant God made with us through Jesus Christ, our permanent reminder — or witness — of the covenant that has been made is the *Holy Spirit*. Romans 8:16 says, "The Spirit itself beareth witness with our spirit, that we are the children of God." Moreover, Paul added, "In whom ye also trusted, after that ye heard the word of truth, the gospel of your salvation: in whom also after that ye believed, ye were sealed with that holy Spirit of promise" (Ephesians 1:13). The Holy Spirit has been given to us as a living witness that we have entered into covenant relationship. He is God's seal of acceptance that has promised to never leave or forsake us.

Taking into account the original Greek meaning, here is the *Renner Interpretive Version* (*RIV*) of Ephesians 1:13:

> **You are also in Him so this applies to you as well, and not just to those who first hoped in Christ. He has also become your permanent residence, dwelling place, habitation, and home. This is what happened to you upon hearing the word of truth, the declaration of the good news which brought you healing, wholeness, restoration, deliverance, well-being, safety, security and protection from all the evil that had been intended for you.**

Friend, you are a covenant partner with Jesus Christ! All of these things have been done for you. Jesus has given you His identity, His authority, His power, His name, His protection, and everything He has is at your disposal. That is why we're told in Romans 8:17, "And if [we are] children, then heirs; heirs of God, and joint-heirs with Christ…." This is not just a feel-good figure of speech. We have been "brothered" with Jesus through His blood and become partakers of His divine nature. In our next lesson, we will look at a gospel-by-gospel comparison of Communion.

STUDY QUESTIONS

Study to shew thyself approved unto God, a workman that needeth not to be ashamed, rightly dividing the word of truth.
— 2 Timothy 2:15

1. Through faith in Christ and the new covenant He provided, we are *exceedingly blessed*! What does God say in Ephesians 1:3 and Second Peter 1:3 about the blessings He provides? Of all the blessings of God He promised in His Word, which ones are you most grateful for? Why are these so precious to you personally?

2. When you repented of your sins and received Christ as your Lord and Savior, you were spiritually reborn as a child of God and received a *spiritual blood transfusion*. You gave Him your sinful, dying blood, and He gave you His perfect, living blood. What does it mean to you to

have Jesus' Blood spiritually coursing through your veins? (Consider Hebrews 9:14; 1 John 1:7; John 6:54-56.)

3. Jesus said, "You can ask him [the Father] for anything, using my name, and I will do it, for this will bring praise to the Father because of what I, the Son, will do for you. Yes, ask anything, using my name, and I will do it!" (John 14:13, 14 *TLB*.) Do you believe this promise from Jesus? Are you praying like this — making bold requests in His Name? If not, why? To strengthen and reignite your faith, consider God's promises to you in John 15:7 and First John 5:14 and 15.

PRACTICAL APPLICATION

> But be ye doers of the word, and not hearers only,
> deceiving your own selves.
> — James 1:22

1. Generally speaking, what has been your attitude toward taking Communion? Why do you partake of it? What do you do to prepare your heart before receiving Communion?

2. After examining the nine components of the covenant and applying them to Communion, what is your most impactful takeaway regarding their significance? How has your perspective on taking Communion changed? How has your Communion experience itself been impacted?

3. Carefully reread the section on the significance of the *covenant meal*. What does this speak to you personally about your relationship with Jesus? How do you see Him differently?

LESSON 3

TOPIC

A Gospel-by-Gospel Comparison

SCRIPTURES

1. **Matthew 26:14-16,20,21,25-28,30** — Then one of the twelve, called Judas Iscariot, went unto the chief priests, and said unto them, What will ye give me, and I will deliver him unto you? And they covenanted with him for thirty pieces of silver. And from that time he sought

opportunity to betray him. Now when the even was come, he sat down with the twelve. And as they did eat, he said, Verily I say unto you, that one of you shall betray me. Then Judas, which betrayed him, answered and said, Master, is it I? He said unto him, Thou hast said. And as they were eating, Jesus took bread, and blessed it, and brake it, and gave it to the disciples, and said, Take, eat; this is my body. And he took the cup, and gave thanks, and gave it to them, saying, Drink ye all of it; For this is my blood of the new testament, which is shed for many for the remission of sins. And when they had sung an hymn, they went out into the mount of Olives.

2. **Matthew 27:3,5** — Then Judas, which had betrayed him, when he saw that he was condemned, repented himself, and brought again the thirty pieces of silver to the chief priests and elders. And he cast down the pieces of silver in the temple, and departed, and went and hanged himself.

3. **Mark 14:10,11** —And Judas Iscariot, one of the twelve, went unto the chief priests, to betray him unto them. And when they heard it, they were glad, and promised to give him money. And he sought how he might conveniently betray him.

4. **Mark 14:17,18,22-24,26** — And in the evening he cometh with the twelve. And as they sat and did eat, Jesus said, Verily I say unto you, One of you which eateth with me shall betray me. And as they did eat, Jesus took bread, and blessed, and brake it, and gave to them, and said, Take, eat: this is my body. And he took the cup, and when he had given thanks, he gave it to them: and they all drank of it. And he said unto them, This is my blood of the new testament, which is shed for many. And when they had sung an hymn, they went out into the mount of Olives.

5. **Luke 22:3-6** — Then entered Satan into Judas surnamed Iscariot, being of the number of the twelve. And he went his way, and communed with the chief priests and captains, how he might betray him unto them. And they were glad, and covenanted to give him money. And he promised, and sought opportunity to betray him unto them in the absence of the multitude.

6. **Luke 22:14,17,19,20,24** — And when the hour was come, he sat down, and the twelve apostles with him. And he took the cup, and gave thanks, and said, Take this, and divide it among yourselves; And he took bread, and gave thanks, and brake it, and gave unto them, saying, This is my body which is given for you: this do in remembrance

of me. Likewise also the cup after supper, saying, This cup is the new testament in my blood, which is shed for you. And there was also a strife among them, which of them should be accounted the greatest.

7. **John 13:1,2,4,5** — Now before the feast of the passover, when Jesus knew that his hour was come that he should depart out of this world unto the Father, having loved his own which were in the world, he loved them unto the end. And supper being ended, the devil having now put into the heart of Judas Iscariot, Simon's son, to betray him; He riseth from supper, and laid aside his garments; and took a towel, and girded himself. After that he poureth water into a bason, and began to wash the disciples' feet, and to wipe them with the towel wherewith he was girded.

8. **John 13:18,21,27-30** — I speak not of you all: I know whom I have chosen: but that the scripture may be fulfilled, He that eateth bread with me hath lifted up his heel against me. When Jesus had thus said, he was troubled in spirit, and testified, and said, Verily, verily, I say unto you, that one of you shall betray me. And after the sop Satan entered into him. Then said Jesus unto him, That thou doest, do quickly. Now no man at the table knew for what intent he spake this unto him. For some of them thought, because Judas had the bag, that Jesus had said unto him, Buy those things that we have need of against the feast; or, that he should give something to the poor. He then having received the sop went immediately out: and it was night.

9. **John 18:1** — When Jesus had spoken these words, he went forth with his disciples over the brook Cedron, where was a garden, into the which he entered, and his disciples.

10. **1 Corinthians 11:23-25, 27** — For I have received of the Lord that which also I delivered unto you, That the Lord Jesus the same night in which he was betrayed took bread: and when he had given thanks, he brake it, and said, Take, eat: this is my body, which is broken for you: this do in remembrance of me. After the same manner also he took the cup, when he had supped, saying, This cup is the new testament in my blood: this do ye, as oft as ye drink it, in remembrance of me. Wherefore whosoever shall eat this bread, and drink this cup of the Lord, unworthily, shall be guilty of the body and blood of the Lord.

GREEK WORDS

1. "shall betray" — **παραδίδωμι** (*paradidomi*): to deliver or hand something over to someone else; in this context, to hand over in the act of betrayal

2. "Master" — **ῥαββί** (*hrabbi*): teacher

3. "testament" — **διαθήκη** (*diatheke*): depicts a covenant made between two people or more

4. "this do" — **τοῦτο ποιεῖτε** (*touto poieite*): this very thing do; emphatically, do this very thing; creatively do; to carry out

5. "remembrance" — **ἀνάμνησις** (*anamnesis*): from **ἀνά** (*ana*) and **μιμνήσκομαι** (*mimneskomai*); the preposition **ἀνά** (*ana*) means "again," as to repeat something over and again; the word **μιμνήσκομαι** (*mimneskomai*) mean to recall or to be mindful; to recall, recollect, or to remember

6. "end" — **τέλος** (*telos*): end; completely; fully; maturely

7. "Satan" — **Σατανᾶς** (*Satanas*): one who hates, accuses, slanders, or conspires against; an adversary

SYNOPSIS

The first mention of the upper room in Jerusalem is in historical Church documents dating back to the Fourth Century. For hundreds of years since then, Christians have come here from far and wide to pray and commune with the Lord and remember all that occurred in this legendary place. As we have seen, the practice of Communion was established by Jesus in the upper room, but what was His purpose? Was He merely giving His disciples a new religious tradition? What exactly did He mean when He commanded "this do in remembrance of Me"? And why is Judas Iscariot mentioned in close connection with the Communion narrative in each gospel's telling?

The emphasis of this lesson:

The first Communion is documented in all four gospels — Matthew, Mark, Luke, and John. Although they all share some of the same details, each offers a unique perspective and provides insights that help connect the ancient components of a covenant with our practice of Communion.

The First Communion –
According to the Gospel of Matthew

Matthew wrote, "Then one of the twelve, called Judas Iscariot, went unto the chief priests, and said unto them, What will ye give me, and I will deliver him unto you? And they covenanted with him for thirty pieces of silver. And from that time he sought opportunity to betray him" (Matthew 26:14-16).

Notice it says that the chief priests "covenanted" with Judas. This is extremely significant. It tells us that just before Judas partook of Communion — the covenant meal — with Jesus, he had already entered into a covenant with the religious leaders. Keep that in mind as we continue.

Matthew went on to say, "Now when the even was come, he sat down with the twelve. And as they did eat, he said, Verily I say unto you, that one of you shall betray me" (Matthew 26:20, 21). The words "shall betray" here is the Greek word *paradidomi*, which means *to deliver or hand something over to someone else*. In this context, it means *to hand over in the act of betrayal*.

The Bible says, "Then Judas, which betrayed him, answered and said, Master, is it I? He said unto him, Thou hast said" (Matthew 26:25). The word "Master" here is the Greek word *hrabbi*, which is the Hebrew equivalent of the Greek word *didaskalos*, meaning *Masterful teacher*. What is interesting is that Judas never addressed Jesus as Lord in any of the gospels. He always called Him Teacher or Rabbi, which tells us Judas had a major flaw in his relationship with Jesus. He only recognized Him as a Teacher but never submitted to Jesus' supreme authority as Lord.

Matthew 26:26 and 27 says, "And as they were eating, Jesus took bread, and blessed it, and brake it, and gave it to the disciples, and said, Take, eat; this is my body. And he took the cup, and gave thanks, and gave it to them, saying, Drink ye all of it." In our previous lessons, we examined the nine components of making a covenant, noting that bread and wine were a key part of the covenant meal. By the giving and breaking of bread, Jesus was telling His disciples, "Everything I have is at your disposal — all My wealth, My possessions, and My body itself." When Jesus shared the wine, it was the equivalent of Him saying, "I give you My life's blood to empower the promises I have just made to you."

Jesus then told the Twelve, "For this is my blood of the new testament, which is shed for many for the remission of sins" (Matthew 26:28). The word "testament" here in Greek is *diatheke*, and it depicts *a covenant made between two people or more*. The use of this word clearly confirms that Jesus was indeed cutting a covenant with His disciples. Matthew 26:30 says, "And when they had sung an hymn, they went out into the mount of Olives."

Although Matthew's gospel does not record Judas' exit from the upper room gathering, we know he left and went to the chief priests with whom he had covenanted. He then led them to Jesus in the Garden of Gethsemane and betrayed the Lord into their hands. What happened to Judas after that? The Bible says, "Then Judas, which had betrayed him, when he saw that he was condemned, repented himself, and brought again the thirty pieces of silver to the chief priests and elders. And he cast down the pieces of silver in the temple, and departed, and went and hanged himself" (Matthew 27:3, 5).

Notice it says Judas "repented himself." The word "repented" is the Greek word *metamelomai*, which actually expresses *sorrow, mourning,* or *grief*. It means *to be seized with guilt; to be filled with remorse or regret*. Although Judas was filled with sorrow for betraying Jesus, he did not repent. True repentance is a change in one's mind and heart that produces a change in one's behavior. Judas was filled with guilt and regret, and it led him to commit suicide.

Why would he take such action? The reason is the components of the covenant were at work. As Judas sat and received the bread and the wine offered by Christ in the upper room, he pretended to make a covenant with Jesus. The truth is, Judas had previously made a covenant with the chief priests. When he partook of the wine and the bread, he did so unworthily, and it broke the terms of his covenant with Jesus. This brought the curses of the covenant down upon him, and he died as a result.

The First Communion –
According to the Gospel of Mark

Mark also wrote about Christ's Communion with the disciples and the events that surrounded it. In Mark 14:10 and 11, it says, "And Judas Iscariot, one of the twelve, went unto the chief priests, to betray him unto them. And when they heard it, they were glad, and promised to give him money. And he sought how he might conveniently betray him."

The Bible goes on to say, "And in the evening he cometh with the twelve. And as they sat and did eat, Jesus said, Verily I say unto you, One of you which eateth with me shall betray me" (Matthew 14:17, 18). Again, the phrase "shall betray" is the Greek word *paradidomi*, which means *to deliver or hand something over to someone else.* In this context, it means *to hand over in the act of betrayal.*

As we saw in Matthew's gospel, during the last supper with His disciples, Jesus also partook of a covenant meal. In Mark's gospel, this begins to unfold in verse 22, which says, "And as they did eat, Jesus took bread, and blessed, and brake it, and gave to them, and said, Take, eat: this is my body. And he took the cup, and when he had given thanks, he gave it to them: and they all drank of it. And he said unto them, This is my blood of the new testament, which is shed for many" (Mark 14:22-24).

We know from our previous lessons that the "cup" represented Jesus' blood, and when a person partook of another person's blood, he or she was partaking of that person's life. Jesus said the cup "…is my blood of the new testament, which is shed for many" (Mark 14:24). The word "testament" here is again the Greek word *diatheke*, which depicts *a covenant made between two people or more.* As Christ and His disciples shared the covenant meal of bread and wine, they became united as one. "And when they had sung an hymn, they went out into the mount of Olives" (Mark 14:26).

The First Communion –
According to the Gospel of Luke

When we come to Luke's account of the first Communion, we hear a reiteration of many of the same facts as well as a few unique insights. As with Matthew and Mark's telling, Luke begins with details concerning Judas. The Bible says, "Then entered Satan into Judas surnamed Iscariot, being of the number of the twelve. And he went his way, and communed with the chief priests and captains, how he might betray him unto them. And they were glad, and covenanted to give him money. And he promised, and sought opportunity to betray him unto them in the absence of the multitude" (Luke 22:3-6).

Again, these verses reveal that Judas "covenanted" with the chief priests. To be clear, these were the religious leaders who despised Jesus and wanted Him out of the way. They promised Judas money in return for him leading them to Jesus when the crowds were not around. One element in Luke's rendition that is different from Matthew and Mark's is his initial statement: "Then entered Satan into Judas… (Luke 22:3)." Something inside Judas' heart and mind was not right, and it had given Satan access to Judas' life, which would soon prove to be his downfall.

The Bible goes on to say, "And when the hour was come, he sat down, and the twelve apostles with him. And he took the cup, and gave thanks, and said, Take this, and divide it among yourselves; And he took bread, and gave thanks, and brake it, and gave unto them, saying, This is my body which is given for you: this do in remembrance of me. Likewise also the cup after supper, saying, This cup is the new testament in my blood, which is shed for you." (Luke 22:14, 17, 19, 20). Here again in these verses we see the components of a covenant.

Take note of what Jesus said at the end of verse 19: "…This do in remembrance of me." This is the only place in the gospels where these words appear, and they are significant. The words "this do" in Greek is *touto poieite*, which means *this very thing do*. It can also be translated *emphatically*, *do this very thing*, or *find a way to creatively do this thing*. The word "remembrance" is also important. It is the Greek word *anamnesis*, which is from the word *ana*, meaning "again," as *to repeat something over and again*; and the word *mimneskomai*, meaning *to recall* or *to be mindful*. Thus, when Jesus said, "This do in remembrance of me," He was saying, "Recall, recollect, and remember what I am doing, and do this very thing."

What is interesting is that Jesus' command was actually twofold. First, He was instructing His disciples — both then and now — to take Communion with each other just as He was doing. He was establishing the practice of Communion as an ordinance of the Church. At the same time, He was also telling the disciples, "Just as you see Me entering into a sacrificial covenant with each of you, I want you to enter into covenant with each other. I want you to be people of covenant, walking in covenant with one another. *This do*, and do it in the same way you see Me doing it." That is a very profound and important truth we need to understand and put into practice.

The First Communion –
According to the Gospel of John

The gospel of John is in a class of its own. A careful reading of its pages reveals a very personal side of Jesus — emphasizing the importance of *relationship* rather than religious ritual. John mentioned the last supper in the upper room in his thirteenth chapter: "Now before the feast of the passover, when Jesus knew that his hour was come that he should depart out of this world unto the Father, having loved his own which were in the world, he loved them unto the end" (John 13:1).

Notice it says that Jesus loved His disciples "unto the end." The word "end" is the Greek word *telos*, which means *the end; completely; fully; maturely.* The use of the word *telos* tells us Jesus loved each of His disciples with the greatest fullness that they could ever receive, all the way to the end of His life.

In John 13:2, John said, "And supper being ended, the devil having now put into the heart of Judas Iscariot, Simon's son, to betray him." This verse is very similar to Luke 22:3. It clearly states, that something wasn't right in Judas' heart, and it opened the door for the devil to enter and inject his poison. He was offended with Jesus and it had festered and turned into bitterness, which gave birth to betrayal in his heart. Judas had no right to sit at the table and partake of the covenant meal with Jesus, yet he did so in an unworthily manner.

John continued by saying, "He [Jesus] riseth from supper, and laid aside his garments; and took a towel, and girded himself. After that he poureth water into a bason, and began to wash the disciples' feet, and to wipe them with the towel wherewith he was girded" (John 13:4,5). The washing of the disciples' feet is only mentioned in John's gospel, and one of the most amazing facts about this event is that Judas was among those whose feet Jesus washed!

Take a moment and imagine the weight of the situation. Judas had already covenanted with the chief priests to turn Jesus over to them. With betrayal in his heart, he sat and received the bread and the wine of the covenant meal with Jesus, all the while knowing what he was about to do. And there was Jesus on His knees washing the feet of the man who sold Him out for thirty pieces of silver. This was the mercy of God being extended to Judas once more, trying to melt his hardened heart and give him opportunity to truly repent. But Judas would not yield.

After Jesus finished washing the disciple's feet, He turned to all His disciples and said, "…He that eateth bread with me hath lifted up his heel against me" (John 13:18). Then verse 21 says, "When Jesus had thus said, he was troubled in spirit, and testified, and said, Verily, verily, I say unto you, that one of you shall betray me." Basically, Jesus told His disciples, "One of you sitting at this table — one of you who just partook of the bread and the wine — has sold Me out. It's one of you who just said you were in covenant with Me, but in truth, you are not in covenant with Me at all. You've already made up your mind to betray Me."

Incredulously, the disciples looked at one another with bewilderment over which of them Jesus was talking about. John questioned Jesus as to who it was. "Jesus answered, He it is, to whom I shall give a sop, when I have dipped it. And when he had dipped the sop, he gave it to Judas Iscariot, the son of Simon. And after the sop Satan entered into him. Then said Jesus unto him, That thou doest, do quickly" (John 13:26,27).

Notice the word "Satan" in verse 27. It is the Greek word *Satanas*, which means *one who hates, accuses, slanders, or conspires against another, an adversary*. The reason Satan had entered into Judas was because Judas gave place to him (*see* Ephesians 4:26, 27). We know for sure that he was indignant with Jesus for allowing the woman to break the expensive bottle of perfume and pour it on His feet (*see* John 12:1-6). It is possible — *even likely* — that this was not the first time Judas was offended with Jesus. In any case, offense lodged in Judas' heart, and he never dealt with it. This hurt became the dirt in which the seeds of betrayal grew.

How did the other disciples respond to all this? The Bible says, "Now no man at the table knew for what intent he spake this unto him. For some of them thought, because Judas had the bag, that Jesus had said unto him, Buy those things that we have need of against the feast; or, that he should give something to the poor" (John 13:28, 29). This was Jesus' perfect opportunity to expose Judas for the betrayer that he was — but He didn't. Instead, Jesus' silence covered the sin which was conceived in Judas' heart. Again, love and mercy was extended to Judas, giving him yet another opportunity to turn and repent. But Judas rejected it. The Bible says, "He [Judas] then having received the sop went immediately out: and it was night" (John 13:30). Symbolically, Judas left the light of the presence of God and entered into not just physical darkness, but eternal darkness.

Remarkably, all of this took place in the upper room of Jerusalem — the last supper, the first Communion, the washing of the disciples' feet, and Jesus' confirmation that Judas was His betrayer. Actually, all the events and discussions found in chapters 14, 15, 16, and 17 of John's gospel all took place in the upper room. It was there that Jesus also announced the coming of the Holy Spirit and shared what His role would be in the lives of believers. It was also the place where Jesus prayed His High Priestly prayer for all His disciples.

The Bible says, "When Jesus had spoken these words, he went forth with his disciples over the brook Cedron, where was a garden, into the which he entered, and his disciples" (John 18:1).

Who Else Talks About Communion in Scripture?

In addition to the four gospel accounts of the first Communion, the apostle Paul also wrote about it in his first letter to the Corinthians. He said, "For I have received of the Lord that which also I delivered unto you, That the Lord Jesus the same night in which he was betrayed took bread: and when he had given thanks, he brake it, and said, Take, eat: this is my body, which is broken for you: this do in remembrance of me. After the same manner also he took the cup, when he had supped, saying, This cup is the new testament in my blood: this do ye, as oft as ye drink it, in remembrance of me. Wherefore whosoever shall eat this bread, and drink this cup of the Lord, unworthily, shall be guilty of the body and blood of the Lord" (1 Corinthians 11:23-25,27). In our next lesson, we will carefully examine this passage and learn what it means to partake of Communion unworthily.

STUDY QUESTIONS

Study to shew thyself approved unto God, a workman that needeth not to be ashamed, rightly dividing the word of truth.
— 2 Timothy 2:15

1. After reading through and carefully examining the four gospel accounts of Jesus serving Communion to His disciples and the events that surrounded it, how has your understanding been expanded?

What do you see that you had not seen before — about Jesus, about Judas, about Communion, and about the upper room?

2. There is a significant distinction between *worldly* sorrow and *godly* sorrow. Carefully read Paul's words in Second Corinthians 7:8-11 and tell how these are different. Both Peter and Judas were deeply sorrowful for failing Jesus. Which one exemplified *worldly* sorrow, and which one exemplified *godly* sorrow? Which kind of sorrow do *you* most often exhibit?

PRACTICAL APPLICATION

But be ye doers of the word, and not hearers only,
deceiving your own selves.
— James 1:22

1. In your own words, briefly describe the meaningful significance of the *bread* and *wine* (or juice) served at a covenant meal (Communion). When you consider all the symbolic meaning of sharing these elements with others, how does it reshape your perspective of taking Communion with fellow church members?

2. The Bible says that Satan gained *entrance* into Judas (*see* Luke 22:3). Carefully read John 12:1-8 and take note of what happened at Lazarus' house just six days before Judas betrayed Jesus. What was Judas' response to Mary's extravagant act of worship toward Jesus? On what was he focused? What lesson(s) can you learn from Judas' life and apply in your own?

3. What does Ephesians 4:26 and 27 say about giving place to the enemy in your life? How do you think Judas' actions relate to this passage? What can you do to effectively close the door on the devil? (Consider God's directive to Cain regarding his response to Abel's worship in Genesis 4:3-7; Paul's instruction in Ephesians 4:30-32; and Jesus words in Mark 11:25, 26.)

TOPIC

What Does It Mean To Be Guilty of the Blood and Body of Jesus?

SCRIPTURES

1. **1 Corinthians 11:23-31** — For I have received of the Lord that which also I delivered unto you, That the Lord Jesus the same night in which he was betrayed took bread: and when he had given thanks, he brake it, and said, Take, eat: this is my body, which is broken for you: this do in remembrance of me. After the same manner also he took the cup, when he had supped, saying, This cup is the new testament in my blood: this do ye, as oft as ye drink it, in remembrance of me. For as often as ye eat this bread, and drink this cup, ye do shew the Lord's death till he come. Wherefore whosoever shall eat this bread, and drink this cup of the Lord, unworthily, shall be guilty of the body and blood of the Lord. But let a man examine himself, and so let him eat of that bread, and drink of that cup. For he that eateth and drinketh unworthily, eateth and drinketh damnation to himself, not discerning the Lord's body. For this cause many are weak and sickly among you, and many sleep. For if we would judge ourselves, we should not be judged.

GREEK WORDS

1. "the same night" — ἐν τῇ νυκτὶ (*en te nukti*): in the very night
2. "betrayed" — παραδίδωμι (*paradidomi*): to deliver or hand something over to someone else; in this context, to hand over in the act of betrayal
3. "this do" — τοῦτο ποιεῖτε (*touto poieite*): this very thing do; emphatically, do this very thing; creatively do; to carry out
4. "remembrance" — ἀνάμνησις (*anamnesis*): from ἀνά (*ana*) and μιμνήσκομαι (*mimneskomai*); the preposition ἀνά (*ana*) means "again," as to repeat something over and again; the word μιμνήσκομαι (*mimneskomai*) mean to recall or to be mindful; to recall, recollect, or to remember

5. "the new testament" — ἡ καινὴ διαθήκη (*he kaine diatheke*): definite article ἡ (*he*) with καινός (*kainos*) and διαθήκη (*diatheke*); the word καινός (*kainos*) depicts something that is absolutely brand new, never known before; the word διαθήκη (*diatheke*) depicts a covenant made between two people or more; as a phrase, the brand-new, never-before-known covenant

6. "oft" — ὁσάκις (*hosakis*): as often; as many times as necessary

7. "often" — ὁσάκις (*hosakis*): as often; as many times as necessary

8. "unworthily" — ἀναξίως (*anaxios*): unworthily; unfit; not equal to the task; not matching the value of the act, honor, position, or task

9. "guilty" — ἔνοχος (*enochos*): liable; indicted; charged; held responsible for a wrong action, behavior, or motive

10. "examine" — δοκιμάζω (*dokimadzo*): test; examine; inspect; scrutinize; determine the quality or sincerity of a thing; the object scrutinized has passed the test, so it can now be viewed as genuine and sincere; used to illustrate tests used to determine real and counterfeit coinage; hence, to approve and deem fit after appropriate testing; also described the process of testing an individual's character to see if he was deemed "fit" for public office; in context, "examine yourself to see if you are in a state of genuine covenant"

11. "damnation" — κρίμα (*krima*): decree; judgment; verdict with an adverse consequence; in this case, the consequences of breaking covenant

12. "not discerning" — μὴ διακρίνων (*me diakrinon*): the word μὴ (*me*) is negative; the word διακρίνω (*diakrino*) depicts one's ability to discern, judge, or be truthful; the word "diakrino" also means to appreciate; in this phrase, one who lacks discernment; one who has no appreciation; one who does not rightly value

13. "weak" — ἀσθενής (*asthenes*): pictures a wide range of infirmities; an all-encompassing term that embraces all forms of sickness, disease, and weaknesses; a wide range of illnesses; can also denote being financially poor; it is also used to convey the idea of something that is fragile and must be treated with supreme care

14. "sickly" — ἄρρωστος (*arrostos*): to be in bad health; to possess a weak and broken condition; pictures a person so weak and sick that he has become critically ill; an invalid; a devastating illness

15. "many" — ἱκανός (*hikanos*): a considerable number; a significant amount

16. "sleep" — **κοιμάομαι** (*koimaomai*): sleep; deep sleep; where we get the word coma; also death

17. "judge" — **διακρίνω** (*diakrino*): depicts one's ability to discern, judge, be truthful, or come under scrutiny; self-scrutiny; self-examination

18. "judged" — **διακρίνω** (*diakrino*): pictures one who has been or is presently suffering consequences of a lack of truthfulness and correcting and valuing of something else

SYNOPSIS

In each of our previous lessons, we have noted that Jesus served Communion to His apostles in the upper room in Jerusalem. The present site was officially authenticated during the Fourth Century, and since then it has been renovated many times, including two massive facelifts during the Eleventh and Fourteenth Centuries. Although there is much history that took place in this room, what is probably most unnerving about it is that it is the actual location where Judas Iscariot faked his allegiance to Jesus and became "guilty of the body and blood of the Lord" (1 Corinthians 11:27). What exactly does this mean, and how can we guard ourselves from committing such an offense?

The emphasis of this lesson:

Judas Iscariot gives us an example of what it means to be guilty of the body and blood of Jesus. There are serious negative repercussions that can result from taking Communion unworthily. To avoid these consequences, we must learn to carefully examine ourselves and know that we are truly living in covenant with God and His people.

Jesus Cut Covenant with His Disciples the Night He Was Betrayed

In addition to the accounts of Communion presented in the four gospels, the apostle Paul also shared a unique and very important perspective of Christ's covenant meal. In First 1 Corinthians 11:23, he began his remarks by stating, "For I have received of the Lord that which also I delivered unto you…." It is interesting to note that the practice of Communion was revealed to Paul by direct revelation from Jesus Himself. No one else schooled him on the subject.

Paul went on to say, "…That the Lord Jesus the same night in which he was betrayed took bread." In the Greek, this verse says, "…*In the very night in which He was betrayed…*." The word "betrayed" is the Greek word *paradidomi*, which means *to deliver* or *hand something over to someone else*. In this context, it means *to hand over in the act of betrayal*. Thus, on *the very same night* Judas Iscariot handed Jesus over to the chief priests and betrayed Him, Jesus shared a covenant meal with His apostles and entered into covenant with them.

The Bible says, "And when he had given thanks, he brake it, and said, Take, eat: this is my body, which is broken for you: this do in remembrance of me" (1 Corinthians 11:24). Jesus' words in this verse are the exact words a person would speak when he or she was making a covenant. "When you partake of this bread," the person would say, "you are partaking of Me and all that I am."

What Jesus Did, We Are To Do

Jesus then said, "…this do in remembrance of me." The words "this do" in Greek are *touto poieite*, and it means *this very thing I want you to do*. Emphatically, it says *do this very thing*. The word *poieite* is from where we get the word *poet*, and it carries with it the idea of *creatively doing something*.

This brings us to the word "remembrance," which is the Greek word *anamnesis*. It is a compound of the preposition *ana*, which means "again," as *to repeat something over and again*; and the word *mimneskomai*, which means *to be mindful* or *to recall, recollect*, or *to remember*. When these words are compounded to form the word *anamnesis*, it means *to recall* or *remember something* and then *do it again and again and again*. This means Jesus wants us to *remember* how He partook of Communion that night and to regularly do the same — not as ritual, but as a lifestyle.

Clearly, Jesus wanted His apostles and all of His followers to remember the new covenant He established, and partaking of Communion would be a continual reminder. But He also wanted His disciples — which includes us — to *emphatically* find a way to enter into covenant relationship with other believers, just as He entered into covenant relationships with those around Him. He said, "By this shall all men know that ye are my disciples, if ye have love one to another" (John 13:35).

Think about it. Jesus sacrificially gave His disciples everything He had. He held nothing back — not even His life's blood. As believers, we are to be covenant people who are sincerely committed to one another, holding nothing back. We are to emphatically and creatively "do" what Jesus did.

Why Did Christ Place an Emphasis on Drinking the Cup?

Paul continued in First Corinthians 11:25 saying, "After the same manner also he took the cup, when he had supped, saying, This cup is the new testament in my blood: this do ye, as oft as ye drink it, in remembrance of me."

Notice the phrase "the new testament." In Greek, it is the words *he kaine diatheke*. This phrase includes the definite article *he*, which means this is not just any covenant — it is *THE* new covenant. The word "new" is from the Greek word *kainos*, which depicts *something that is absolutely brand new, never known before*. And the word "testament" is the Greek word *diatheke*, which describes *a covenant made between two people or more*. When these three words come together as a phrase, it means *the brand new, never-before-known, covenant*. Jesus was making a brand new, never-before-known covenant, and it was a covenant in His own blood.

Then Christ added, "...This do ye, as oft as ye drink it, in remembrance of me" (1 Corinthians 11:25). The words "this do" are once again the Greek phrase *touto poiete*, which means *this very thing do*; *emphatically do this very thing*; or find a way to creatively do what I am doing. The word "oft" in Greek is the word *hosakis*, and it means *as often* or *as many times as necessary*.

It is interesting to note that Jesus didn't say, "As oft as you eat the bread." He placed emphasis on drinking the cup. This signifies that you are going to have to drink of the cup again and again and again. It indicates making a commitment to give yourself to someone over and over and over again — placing everything that is yours at their disposal. In other words, this is not a one-time event; it is a long-term commitment.

To faithfully keep such a commitment, you will need the empowering life of Jesus — represented by the cup — and you will need to drink of it again and again and again. Symbolically, it means drinking from the cup of sacrifice. Some relationships will require constant sacrifice to maintain peace and unity and stay in covenant fellowship. Your marriage to your spouse and your relationship with God are two such examples.

Jesus said we are to do this in "remembrance" of Him. The word "remembrance" is again the Greek word *anamnesis*, which means *to recall, to recollect*, or *to be mindful of something and to repeat it over and again*. This is the equivalent of Jesus saying, "Remember what I did for you. I didn't just hand you bread to eat; I gave you the cup of wine as well. I paid the ultimate price and went to the Cross, giving My life's blood to empower My promise and place all that is Mine at your disposal. I want you to recall to mind what I did and in the same way sacrificially give of yourself for others."

In First Corinthians11:26, Paul said, "For as often as ye eat this bread, and drink this cup, ye do shew the Lord's death till he come." The word "often" here is from the same root at the word "oft" in verse 25. It is the Greek word *hosakis*, which means *as often* or *many times*. This indicates we are to participate in the practice of Communion regularly, and every time we partake of the bread and wine (or juice), we are to remember our covenant with Christ and all He did for us. Again, taking Communion is also to remind us to do for others just as Jesus did for us. We are to live sacrificially — especially to our brothers and sisters in the Church.

Don't Take Communion 'Unworthily'

Then in First Corinthians 11:27, Paul gave us this sobering warning about receiving Communion: "Wherefore whosoever shall eat this bread, and drink this cup of the Lord, unworthily, shall be guilty of the body and blood of the Lord."

The word "unworthily" in this verse is the Greek word *anaxios*, which means *unworthily, unfit, not equal to the task*. This word carries the idea of *not matching the value of the act, honor, position, or task*. The fact that the Holy Spirit moved on Paul to write this warning tells us that some people who come to the Lord's Table are *unfit* to take Communion — their character does not match the value or honor of receiving the elements representing the body and blood of Jesus. These are individuals who say the right thing with their lips, but the actions of their life speak differently.

This describes Judas Iscariot on the night of the last supper. He sat at the table with the rest of the disciples and pretended to enter into covenant with Jesus, but he was already in covenant with Jesus' enemies. Satan had entered Judas' heart and sown seeds of betrayal, and in that poisoned state, he ate the bread and drank of the cup as if nothing was wrong. His actions were *unworthy*, and he became guilty of the body and blood of the Lord.

The word "guilty" in Greek is the word *enochos*, which describes *someone liable; indicted;* or *charged.* This is *a person who is held responsible for a wrong action, behavior, or motive.* Clearly, God looks at taking Communion very seriously, and so should we. It is not just the elements we need to understand; we need to understand the meaning of the holy covenant Communion represents. By receiving the bread and wine (or juice), we are saying we are in covenant with God and with one another. If you are not living as a covenant-keeping believer, you should not partake of Communion.

Take Time To Examine Yourself

What are you to do to avoid the danger of partaking of Communion unworthily? Paul said, "But let a man examine himself, and so let him eat of that bread, and drink of that cup" (1Corinthians11:28). The word "examine" in Greek is the word *dokimadzo*, and it means *to test, examine,* or *inspect.* It can also be translated *to scrutinize* or *determine the quality or sincerity of a thing.* Once the object (or person) being scrutinized has passed the test, it can now be viewed as genuine and sincere. This word *dokimadzo* was used to illustrate *tests used to determine real and counterfeit coinage.* It was also used to describe *the process of testing an individual's character to see if they were deemed "fit" for public office.*

In the context of this verse, the word *dokimadzo* means to examine yourself to see if you are in a state of genuine covenant — are you actually living up to the terms of the new covenant in Christ's blood and spiritually fit to partake of Communion. To be clear, this is not about behaving perfectly. It is about being in good standing with God and others through repentance and faith in Christ. This means when the Holy Spirit convicts you of something that is out of line, you deal with it quickly; you don't sweep it under the rug.

Paul went on to say, "For he that eateth and drinketh unworthily, eateth and drinketh damnation to himself, not discerning the Lord's body" (1 Corinthians 11:29). The word "damnation" is the Greek word *krima*, which describes *a decree; a judgment;* or *a verdict with an adverse consequence.* Just as there are natural laws that cannot be broken, there are also spiritual laws to which we must adhere. If you break a spiritual law, which in this case is breaking covenant, there are certain consequences.

Hence, if you partake of the bread and the cup with an insincere heart that is not honoring the Lord and upholding His covenant, you bring a judgment upon yourself for "…not discerning the Lord's body" (1 Corinthians 11:29). The words "not discerning" in Greek depict *one's inability to discern, to judge, to appreciate,* or *to be truthful.* In this phrase, it describes *one who lacks discernment; one who has no appreciation; one who does not rightly value Christ's sacrificial covenant.*

The Repercussions of Partaking of Communion Unworthily

As we saw in our previous lessons, one of the components of a covenant is *blessings and curses.* A person who maintained their part of the covenant reaped blessings. However, if he or she broke their covenant commitment, they experienced adverse consequences. In the same way, people who receive the bread and the cup and pretend to be in covenant relationship with God and His people but are not living up to the covenant terms, they will reap negative repercussions.

Specifically, the apostle Paul wrote, "For this cause many are weak and sickly among you, and many sleep" (1 Corinthians 11:30). Notice the word "many." It is the Greek word *polus,* which indicates *great numbers.* The Bible says that *great numbers* of people are "weak and sickly" because they have taken Communion unworthily.

The word "weak" here is the Greek word *asthenes,* which describes *a wide range of infirmities;* it is *an all-encompassing term that embraces all forms of sickness, disease, and weaknesses.* It depicts *a wide range of illnesses* and can also denote being *financially poor.* This word is also used to convey *the idea of something that is fragile and must be treated with supreme care.*

This brings us to the word "sickly," which is the Greek word *arroustos,* and it means *to be in bad health; to possess a weak and broken condition.* This depicts *a person so weak and sick that he has become critically ill.* It can even refer to *an invalid.*

Not only are "many" weak and sickly, but many also "sleep." This word "sleep" is the Greek word *koimaomai,* and it describes *sleep* or *a deep sleep.*

Moreover, it is the word from which we get the word *coma*. The word *koimaomai* can also refer to *death*.

Keep in mind that this strong warning about receiving Communion was written by the apostle Paul to the Corinthian church. At that time they were embroiled in bitter fighting, jealously, and divisions. They were even taking one other to court and suing each other. And in that condition, they were partaking of Communion. They claimed to be in covenant with God and one another, but their behavior demonstrated just the opposite. They were not living up to the terms of the covenant, and therefore were taking Communion unworthily and reaping dreadful consequences.

Paul urged them — and he urges us — to examine themselves. In First Corinthians 11:31, he added, "For if we would judge ourselves, we should not be judged." The word "judge" here is the Greek word *diakrino*, which depicts *one's ability to discern, judge, be truthful,* or *to come under scrutiny.* Hence, if we will be truthful and take a scrutinizing look at our attitudes, our thoughts, and our actions, we will not be "judged," meaning we will not be one who has been or is presently suffering consequences of a lack of truthfulness and correcting or valuing of something else.

Friend, receiving Communion is a very serious matter. It is about being in covenant with God and in covenant with His people, and we should never partake of it haphazardly. Before you take Communion, take time to soberly examine yourself to see if you are *in* or *out* of covenant with God and His Church. Repent of anything that is keeping you from being in sync and living in unity with others. And then you can partake of Communion with confidence that the Lord's life will fill and supernaturally empower you for His service.

STUDY QUESTIONS

Study to shew thyself approved unto God, a workman that needeth not to be ashamed, rightly dividing the word of truth.
— 2 Timothy 2:15

1. The life that Jesus lived was *selfless*. He Himself said, "…[I] did not come to be served, but to serve, and to give my life as a ransom for many" (Mark 10:45 *TLB*). Carefully read what Jesus said in Luke 9:23 and 24 along with Paul's words in Galatians 2:20 and Romans

12:1, and in your own words tell how these passages embody living a covenant life.

2. Imagine you are trying to relay what you just learned in this lesson to a very close friend. In your own words, how would you explain what it means to partake of Communion "unworthily"? How does the life of Judas Iscariot factor into this? Why does the Holy Spirit warn us so strong against this?

PRACTICAL APPLICATION

But be ye doers of the word, and not hearers only,
deceiving your own selves.
— James 1:22

1. When Jesus cut covenant with His disciples, which includes us, He held nothing back — not even His life's blood. Although God is not asking you to *physically* sacrifice your life for someone, He will ask you to sacrificially give of your time, your attention, and your resources. Who is the Holy Spirit bringing to your mind right now in which He wants you to sacrificially invest? What specifically is He asking you to give and/or do for them?

2. Take time to soberly *examine yourself* and see if you are *in* or *out* of covenant with God and His Church. Ask the Holy Spirit to show you the attitudes and motives of your heart, the condition of your mind, and the quality of your actions. Are there any areas where you are not keeping covenant? Repent of anything He reveals that would cause you to be unworthy of receiving Communion.

TOPIC
The Supernatural Element in Communion

SCRIPTURES

1. **1 Corinthians 10:14, 16-22** — Wherefore, my dearly beloved, flee from idolatry. The cup of blessing which we bless, is it not the Communion of the blood of Christ? The bread which we break, is it not the Communion of the body of Christ? For we being many are one bread, and one body: for we are all partakers of that one bread. Behold Israel after the flesh: are not they which eat of the sacrifices partakers of the altar? What say I then? that the idol is any thing, or that which is offered in sacrifice to idols is any thing? But I say, that the things which the Gentiles sacrifice, they sacrifice to devils, and not to God: and I would not that ye should have fellowship with devils. Ye cannot drink the cup of the Lord, and the cup of devils: ye cannot be partakers of the Lord's table, and of the table of devils. Do we provoke the Lord to jealousy? are we stronger than he?

GREEK WORDS

1. "flee" — φεύγω (*pheugo*): flee; to take flight; to run away; to run as fast as possible; to escape; pictures one's feet flying as he runs from a situation

2. "cup of blessing" — Τὸ ποτήριον τῆς εὐλογίας (*To poterion tes eulogias*): Literally, the cup of thanksgiving; the word εὐλογίας (*eulogias*) is a compound of εὖ (*eu*) and λόγος (*logos*); the word εὖ (*eu*) conveys the idea of something wonderful; the word λόγος (*logos*) means words; compounded, pictures a heart and mouth overflowing with good words; blessing; thanksgiving; where we get the word "Eucharist"

3. "Communion"— κοινωνία (*koinonia*): from the word κοινός (*koinos*), which refers to things that are common or mutually shared, such as property that jointly belongs to two or more people; the idea of commonality or connectedness is intrinsic to the meaning of this word; when κοινός (*koinos*) develops into the word κοινωνός (*koinonos*), it

conveys the ideas of engagement, involvement, fellowship, or participation

4. "partakers" — μετέχω (*metecho*): to actively partake of; to be an actual participant

5. "partakers" — κοινωνία (*koinonia*): from the word κοινός (*koinos*), which refers to things that are common or mutually shared, such as property that jointly belongs to two or more people; the ideas of commonality or connectedness is intrinsic to the meaning of this word; when κοινός (*koinos*) develops into the word κοινωνός (*koinonos*), it conveys the ideas of engagement, involvement, fellowship, or participation

6. "devils" — δαιμόνιον (*daimonion*): evil spirits; demons; devils

7. "ye should have" — γίνομαι (*ginomai*): something that occurs over the passage of time

8. "fellowship" — κοινωνός (*koinonos*): from the word κοινός (*koinos*), which refers to things that are common or mutually shared, such as property that jointly belongs to two or more people; the idea of commonality or connectedness is intrinsic to the meaning of this word; when κοινός (*koinos*) develops into the word κοινωνός (*koinonos*), it conveys the ideas of engagement, involvement, fellowship, or participation

9. "table" — τράπεζα (trapedza): table; banqueting table; bank

SYNOPSIS

Today, people from all around the world journey to Jerusalem to visit the upper room to commune with the Lord and experience His presence. We know from Scripture that this was the place where the Holy Spirit was first poured out on the 120 disciples that were united in prayer on the day of Pentecost. It was also the place where Jesus initiated the practice of Communion, serving His disciples the very night He was betrayed. From the birth of the Church in Acts 2 forward, Communion has been regularly observed among the saints even to this day.

In our last lesson, we learned what it means to take Communion unworthily and be guilty of the body and blood of Jesus. We saw in Paul's first letter to the Corinthians how he warned them — and us — to carefully examine ourselves before partaking of the bread and the wine (or juice). History reveals that the believers in Corinth at that time were bickering and fighting with one another and the level of strife among them had become so volatile that they were taking each other to court and suing one another.

Amazingly, these same contentious believers were going to church and taking Communion. As a result, many of them were sick, weak, and some had even died. They were not living as people of covenant. They were breaking a spiritual law and reaping the consequences of their behavior. Instead of walking in love and mercy and patiently forgiving one another as Jesus had instructed, they were filled with anger and bitterness, and therefore unfit to partake of the Lord's Table. This demonstrates the seriousness of taking Communion with a right heart.

The emphasis of this lesson:

To those walking in covenant relationship with God and His people, the table of Communion is a storehouse of great blessings.

Flee Spiritually Dark Environments

In the tenth chapter of First Corinthians, the apostle Paul gave a strong warning about Communion. In verse 14 he urged his listeners to "… flee from idolatry." The word "flee" here is the Greek word *pheugo*, which means *to take flight*; *to run away*; *to run as fast as possible*; or *to escape*. It pictures *one's feet flying as he runs from a situation*. The reason Paul included the subject of idolatry in connection with Communion is because idolatry proliferated the landscape in the ancient world, and where sacrifices were being made to idols, demon spirits were present in large numbers.

Although the idols themselves were nothing more that carved wood or stone, the dark environment where the idol worship was taking place was spiritually charged with evil spirits. Under the guidance of the priests and priestesses serving in these pagan temples, the spirit realm was stirred up, and demon spirits were magnetically drawn to these grounds.

Why was this significant to New Testament believers? Because in the First Century, the finest cuts of meat were sold inside of near pagan temples. Consequently, many believers were entering these sinful shrines to purchase meat, and thereby exposing themselves to intense demonic activity. As a result of this exposure, some began to fall back under the old influences from which they had been delivered. They would enter free and leave demonically oppressed.

Paul knew that being physically close to those spiritually dark environments was too great a risk for these believers, so he urged them to stay away from those sites. Basically, he said, "Buy your meat from somewhere else, or don't eat meat at all. Meat is just not that important." Demonic oppression is a very high price to pay for finding a quality cut of meat, which is why he wrote, "Wherefore, my dearly beloved, flee from idolatry" (1 Corinthians 10:14).

Communion is a 'Cup of Blessing'

Paul went on to say, "The cup of blessing which we bless, is it not the Communion of the blood of Christ? The bread which we break, is it not the Communion of the body of Christ?" (1 Corinthians 10:16). The phrase "cup of blessing" in Greek is *To poterion tes eulogias*, and it literally means *the cup of thanksgiving*. The word *eulogias* is a compound of the words *eu* and *logos*. The word *eu* conveys the idea of *something wonderful*; the word *logos* means *words*. When these two words are compounded to form *eulogias*, it pictures *a heart and mouth overflowing with good words*, *blessing*, and *thanksgiving*. The word *eulogias is from* where we get the word "Eucharist," meaning Communion.

This brings us to the word "Communion," which in this verse is the Greek word *koinonia*. It is from the word *koinos*, which refers to *things that are common* or *mutually shared*, such as property that jointly belongs to two or more people. The idea of *commonality* or *connectedness* is intrinsic to the meaning of this word. When *koinos* develops into the word *koinonos*, it conveys the ideas of *engagement*, *involvement*, *fellowship*, or *participation*. The use of this word tells us that when we partake of Communion, we experience real engagement or participation with the body and blood of Christ.

In the next verse, Paul added, "For we being many are one bread, and one body: for we are all partakers of that one bread" (1 Corinthians 10:17). The word "partakers" here is the Greek word *metecho*, which means *to actively partake of, to be an actual participant*. Paul's use of this word indicates that in order to experience the benefits of Communion, we must actively invest our faith as we receive the elements.

Paul Urged Us Not To Have 'Fellowship with Devils'

Then Paul said, "Behold Israel after the flesh: are not they which eat of the sacrifices partakers of the altar?" (1 Corinthians 10:18). In this verse, Paul is actually talking about the Jewish priests who served in the temple. Essentially, they spent most of their waking hours serving, eating, and living near the altar, which means they were "partakers" of the altar in constant contact with the presence of God. He states this fact and then gives the Corinthians an illustration from the pagan world in the next two verses to help them understand.

> **"What say I then? that the idol is any thing, or that which is offered in sacrifice to idols is any thing? But I say, that the things which the Gentiles sacrifice, they sacrifice to devils, and not to God: and I would not that ye should have fellowship with devils" (1 Corinthians 10:19, 20).**

Initially, Paul stated the fact that an idol is nothing and has no power whatsoever. Likewise, sacrifices made to the idols are also of no consequence. However, behind every idol is an evil spiritual presence. He called them "devils," which is the Greek word *daimonion*, and it describes *evil spirits, demons, or devils.*

Knowing the seriousness of the situation, Paul urged, "…I would not that ye should have fellowship with devils" (1 Corinthians 10:19, 20). The phrase "ye should have" is a translation of the Greek word *ginomai*, which describes *something that occurs over the passage of time.* By using this word, Paul was saying, "I don't want you to progressively be influenced or draw closer and closer in fellowship with evil spirits."

The word "fellowship" is again the Greek word *koinonos*, which is from the word *koinos*, and it refers to *things that are common or mutually shared, such as property that jointly belongs to two or more people.* This word intrinsically carries the idea of *commonality* or *connectedness.* When *koinos* develops into the word *koinonos*, it conveys the ideas of *engagement, involvement, fellowship, or participation.* Paul used this word a second time to inform the Corinthian believers that when they went into pagan temples where sacrifices were being offered to idols, they placed themselves in danger of becoming engaged and involved with demons. Hence, a person's physical presence in the proximity of idol worship put him or her at risk of coming under the influence of the demonic realm. For some this would happen rather quickly, and for others it would have been more progressive (*ginomai*).

Putting the meanings of these words together, here is the *Renner Interpretive Version* (*RIV*) for the second part of 1 Corinthians 10:20:

> **...And I would not that ye should have participation with devils as a result of being in the atmosphere of idolatrous sacrifices and activities.**

We Must Choose From Which Table We Will Eat

To all this, Paul added, "Ye cannot drink the cup of the Lord, and the cup of devils: ye cannot be partakers of the Lord's table, and of the table of devils" (1 Corinthians 10:21). The word "partakers" here is again the Greek word *metecho*, which we saw in verse 17. It means *to actively partake of* or *to be an actual participant*. The placement of this word here indicates that one cannot actively participate and partake of the sacrifices made to evil spirits and at the same time actively participate and partake of the Lord's Communion. In other words, we can't live for God and Satan at the same time.

Friend, you must choose from which table you will eat. You can either be in covenant with God partake of the Lord's Table, or you can be in covenant with Satan and feed on the things of this world. Realize that just as demonic spirits permeated the presence of pagan temples where sacrifices were made to idols, they also hover around people and places devoted to the deeds of darkness. If you choose to expose yourself to these dark influences, you are precariously placing yourself in great danger.

The great news is that God's Holy Spirit permeates the presence around the table of Communion. This brings us to the word "table" in First Corinthians 10:21, which in Greek is the word *trapedza*, and it describes a *table*; *banqueting table*; or a *bank*. Paul's use of this word tells us that just as a bank is loaded with all the resources a person would ever need, the Lord's Table is loaded with spiritual resources, and one can make withdrawals whenever needed. Basically, Communion is a storehouse rich in deliverance, healing, forgiveness, and every other form of grace you need. If your heart is right and you come in faith, you have instant access to the Lord's supernatural abundance.

Make no mistake: our God is a jealous God (*see* James 4:5). He yearns for your undivided affection and will not settle for anything less than having first place in your life. It is no wonder the apostle Paul posed the question, "Do we provoke the Lord to jealousy? are we stronger than he?" (1 Corinthians 10:22). Indeed, this is a sobering question that shows just how serious taking Communion is in God's sight.

Now you may ask, "Well, what if I've made mistakes? What if I've been unfaithful in my covenant relationship with God? How am I supposed to respond if I'm frustrated and aggravated with my spouse or my children or someone in the Church? Can I never partake of Communion?" Of course not. You are a child of God, regardless of your behavior. He doesn't want you to abandon Communion. He simply wants you to examine your heart and get things right before participating. If you've sinned, confess your sin. The Bible says, "If we confess our sins, he is faithful and just to forgive us our sins, and to cleanse us from all unrighteousness" (1 John 1:9). Likewise, if you are offended with someone, choose to drop it and ask God to forgive you for holding onto unforgiveness. Receive His forgiveness and pray for the ones who hurt you.

Once you have made things right with God in your heart, come to the Lord's Table in faith believing to be blessed. In faith, eat the bread and drink the cup, believing God to provide whatever you need. Receiving the elements of Communion releases supernatural provisions of healing, restoration, strength, wisdom, favor, peace, and anything else you need to live a life worthy of His calling.

STUDY QUESTIONS

Study to shew thyself approved unto God, a workman that needeth not to be ashamed, rightly dividing the word of truth.
— 2 Timothy 2:15

1. Exposing yourself to evil influences can be hazardous to your spiritual health. God gives us ample wisdom in His Word to help us avoid the scenes of temptation. What related insights can you identify and apply to your life from Proverbs 5:3-8; Psalm 101:3; and 1 Corinthians 6:18?

2. The apostle Paul pointedly talks about the kind of company we keep in Second Corinthians 6:14-18. Take time to reflect on this passage

and listen for what the Holy Spirit speaks to you. Are there any adjustments you need to make in who you're hanging out with? (Also consider Proverbs 13:20; 22:24, 25; 1 Corinthians 15:33.)

PRACTICAL APPLICATION

**But be ye doers of the word, and not hearers only,
deceiving your own selves.
—James 1:22**

1. Although most of us do not live in places where idol worship is practiced, these truths are still relevant. Given your living environment and what you are subject to, how can you apply these principles in your life?

2. What specific people, places, or things do you know you need to avoid because they would tempt you to fall back into old sinful patterns and habits from which Christ has already delivered you?

3. The Lord's Table of Communion is like a *spiritual bank*. When your heart is right, you can partake of Communion in faith and make a withdrawal of whatever you need. What do you need from the Lord right now? Is it healing? Is it wisdom to handle a certain situation? Is it financial provision? Take time to prepare your heart in prayer, receive Communion, and boldly ask God for what you need.

www.ingramcontent.com/pod-product-compliance
Lightning Source LLC
Chambersburg PA
CBHW051048030426
42339CB00006B/250